For all my dear loved ones,
past and present.

© Rayner Tapia, 2025

All rights reserved. No part of this book may be reproduced or utilised in any form or by any means, electronic or mechanical, including photocopying, recording, or by any information storage and retrieval system, without permission in writing from the author.

First published in 2025
Written by Rayner Tapia
Illustrated by Marian Marinov
Book design by Bryony Simmonds

ISBN: 978-1-915495-77-8 (hardcover)

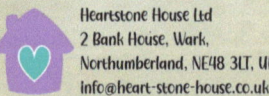

Heartstone House Ltd
2 Bank House, Wark,
Northumberland, NE48 3LT, UK
info@heart-stone-house.co.uk

DISCLAIMER: The *Harry the Hedgehog* series is a work of fiction intended for children. Any resemblance to real persons, living or deceased, is purely coincidental. The characters, events, and settings in this book are products of the author's imagination and are not meant to represent any real individuals, organisations, or places.

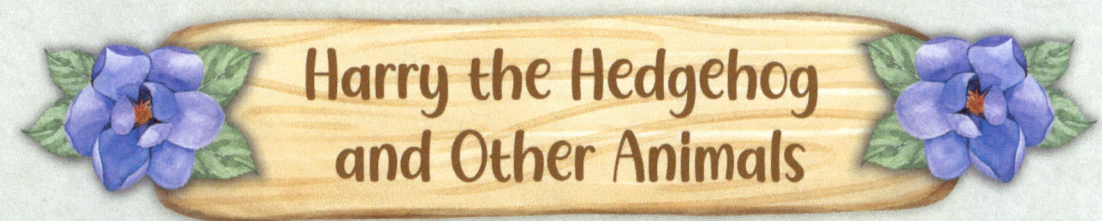

Harry the Hedgehog and Other Animals

Harry the Hedgehog's Harvest

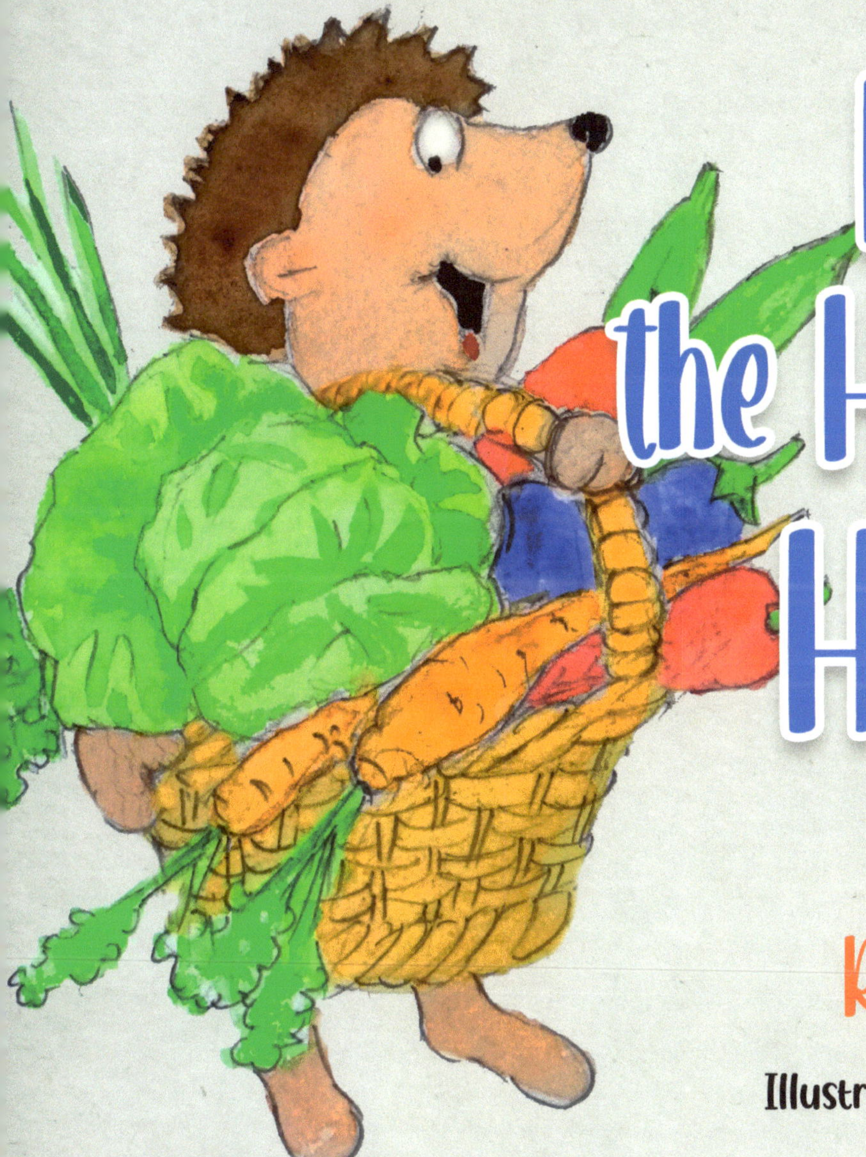

Written by Rayner Tapia

Illustrated by Marian Marinov

Autumn had arrived in the garden. Crunch, scrunch, crunch went the leaves under tiny paws. The air was crisp. Whoosh went the breeze.

Golden leaves twirled and tumbled to the ground. It was time for the annual harvest festival!

Harry the Hedgehog pitter-pattered through the large garden, eager to help. His best friends, Danny the Dog and Milo the Teddy Bear Dog bounded beside him, *tails wag-wag-wagging* with excitement.

Milo, the Teddy Bear Dog, licked his snout and bounced, bounced, bounced up and down.

"Ehm, woof! Harvest Day has come!" he yipped excitedly.

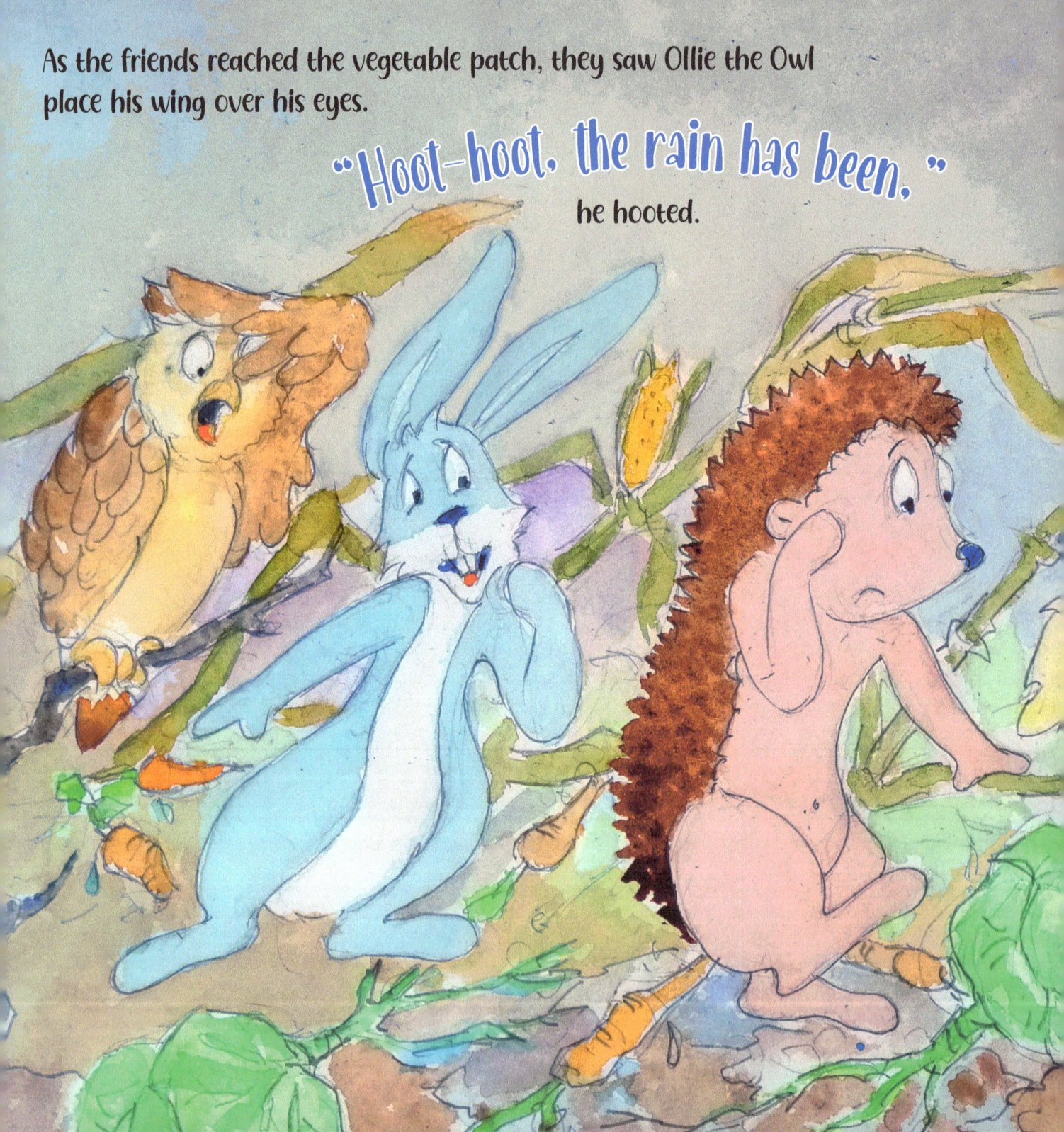

As the friends reached the vegetable patch, they saw Ollie the Owl place his wing over his eyes.

"Hoot-hoot, the rain has been," he hooted.

Suzy the Squirrel twitched her bushy tail.

"The rain came pitter-pattering too hard, washing away many of the acorns and seeds," she sighed.

"Now there are so few nuts to gather," Suzy the Squirrel sniffed. "The harvest festival won't be the same."

Harry the Hedgehog huffed and puffed. "We must do something. Chuff-chuff...snuff!"

Milo wagged his soft, brown, curly tail. "Woof! What if we help plant more?"

Milo's fluffy ears perked up. "We can dig and plant together for a big harvest next time!" he barked, his paws pat-pattering with excitement.

The animals cheered.

Clap-clap!

They hadn't thought about replanting.

Harry the Hedgehog, Danny the Dog, and Milo the Teddy Bear Dog got to work. Harry used his little paws to pat and push seeds into the soil.

pat, pat, push.

Danny the Dog dug small holes with his strong paws, scratching and making space for new roots to grow.

Dig, scratch, burrow.

"Woof! Woof! Look what I found - my bone from yesterday!" he yipped excitedly.

Milo the Teddy Bear Dog carried water from the stream, splashing along to make sure the seeds had plenty to drink.

Splish, splash, splosh.

The rabbits helped, too, nibbling away weeds to clear space for new plants.

Nibble, nibble, nibble!

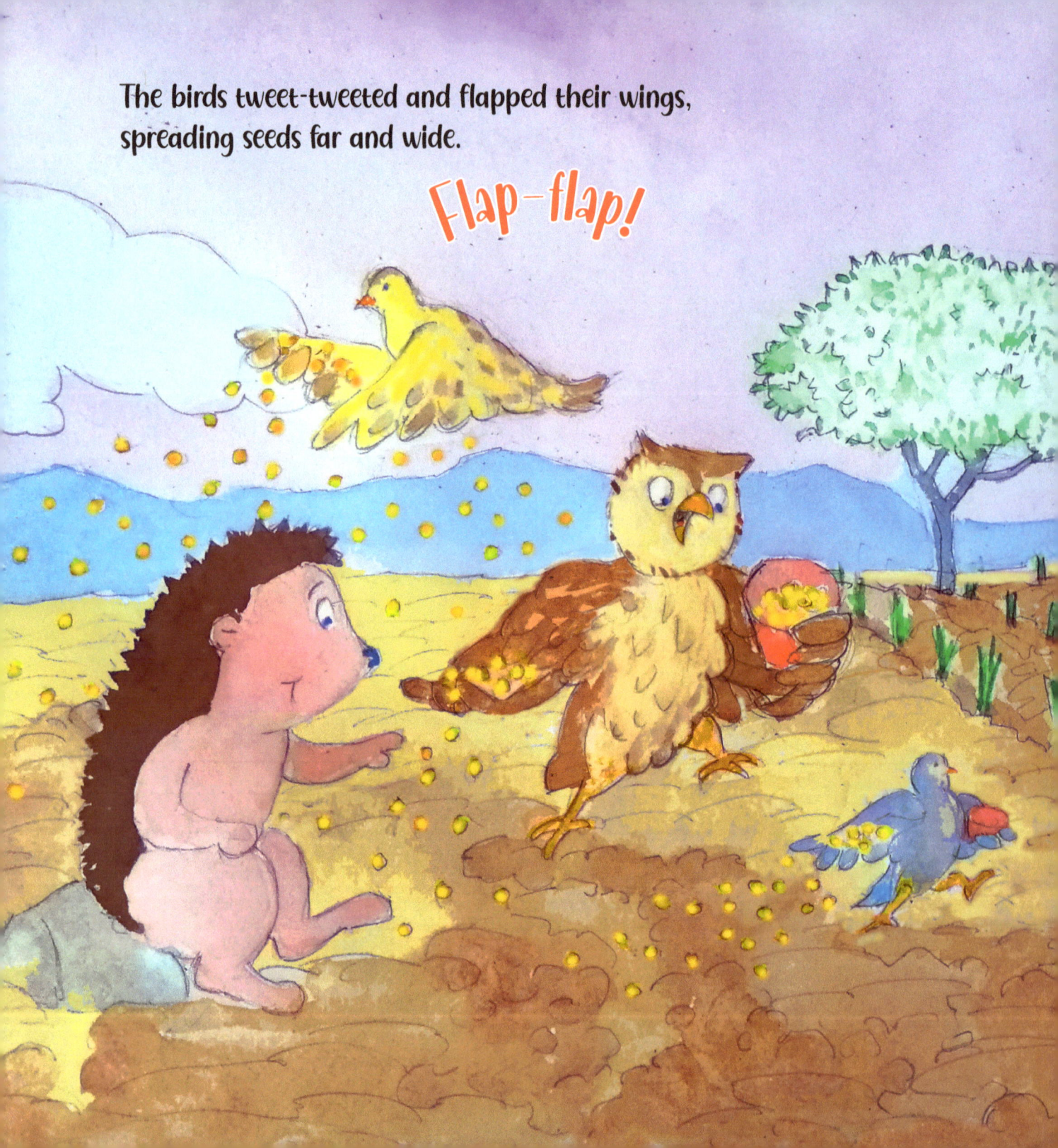
The birds tweet-tweeted and flapped their wings, spreading seeds far and wide.

Flap-flap!

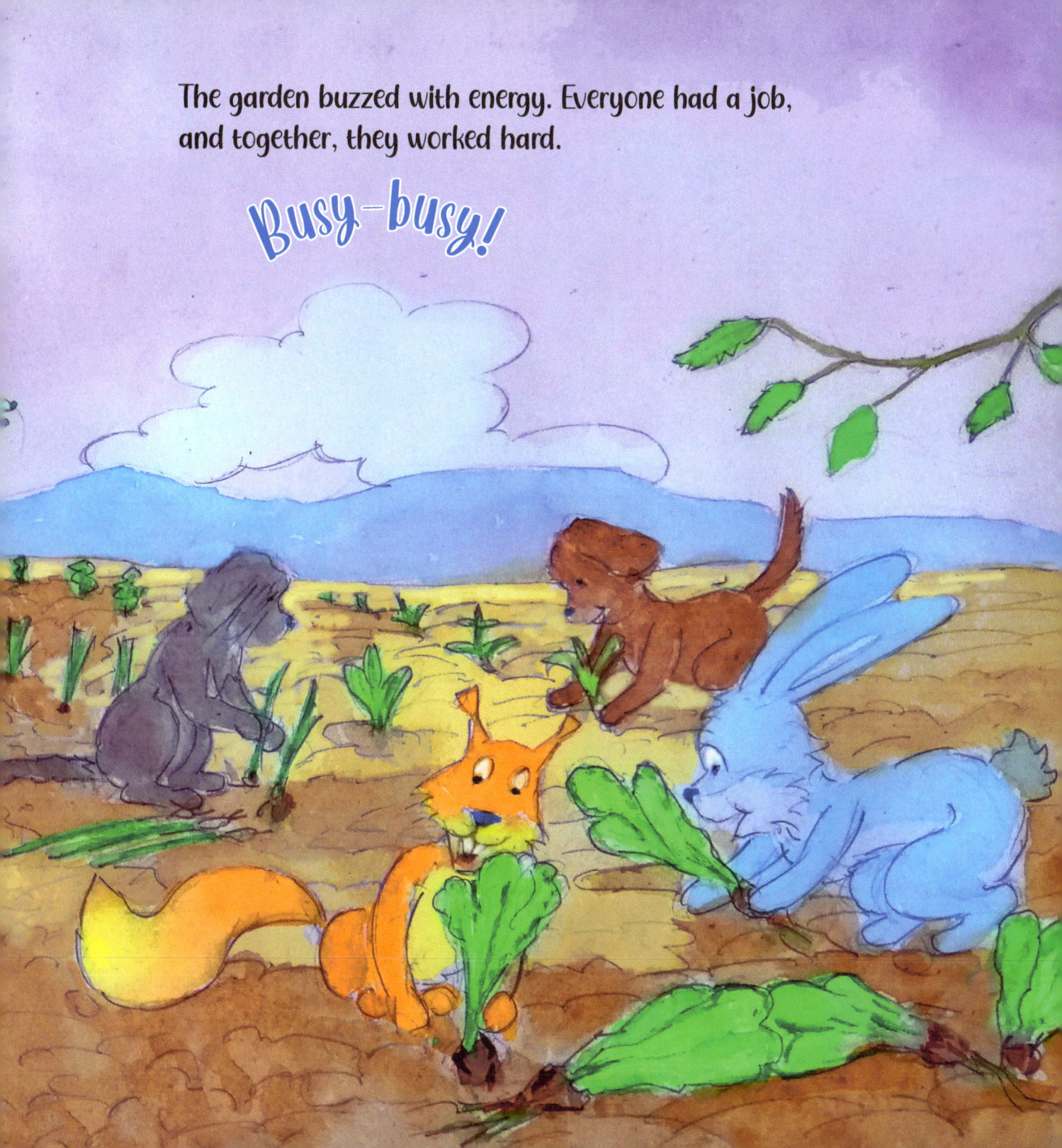

The garden buzzed with energy. Everyone had a job, and together, they worked hard.

Busy-busy!

Days passed, and little green sprouts started to peek through the soil.

Pop-pop!

"We did it!"

Milo barked happily. "The plants are growing! Woof! Woof!"

Harry the Hedgehog nodded. "Chuff-chuff, it may take time, but by the next harvest, the plants will have big, bright, tasty fruit!"

Many weeks later, the garden patch was full of golden corn, plump peas, and juicy berries. Plop-plop went the ripe fruits as they were picked.

The animals gathered around, amazed at how much had grown.

"Hooray!" they cheered.

Clap-clap!

"This is our best harvest yet!" chattered Suzy the Squirrel merrily.

Danny the Dog wagged his tail proudly. "Woof! Woof! Working together made all the difference!"

Milo the Teddy Bear Dog grinned. "Woof! Woof! Yes, it's because *we worked with kindness!*"

That evening, the animals celebrated under the twinkling sparkling stars.

Twinkle-twinkle!

As laughter filled the air, the animals knew they had more than enough for the next harvest.

Not just food but friendship, kindness, and joy.

Giggle-giggle!

The friends curled up beside Harry the Hedgehog, their hearts full and happy. Snuggle-snuggle!

Ollie the Owl hooted, "Twit-ahoo!

Working together makes everything all right."

So, by helping each other and working together with kindness, everything becomes easier, and even the toughest challenges are overcome.

Hip-hip-hooray!

The End

About the Author

Rayner Tapia is one of the NABE Pinnacle Book Achievement winners; The Dream Catcher won the 2012 NABE for Best Juvenile Fiction Books. NABE winner 2016 Best Sci-fiction book and honorary award for Literature, Florida. Rayner Tapia lives in London with her family. She is an IT trainer/teacher for children and adults. She recently (2019) passed English with Distinction, CPD, 2-4 Teaching Literacy in Schools. She is a published author and entrepreneur. Rayner has worked in banking, and has taught IT and English.

Other books by the Author

The Mouse Series

The Mouse and the Fox
The Mouse and the Christmas Tree
The Mouse and the King's Birthday Cake
The Mouse, the Llama, and the Sheep
The Mouse and the Bear
The Mouse and the Seal
Mouse goes on Safari
The Mouse and the Zebra
The Mouse is a Friend indeed
The Mouse goes Home

The Harry the Hedgehog Series

Harry the Hedgehog Saves the Day
Harry the Hedgehog meets Danny the Dog
Harry the Hedgehog meets Charlie the Crane
Harry the Hedgehog and the Missing Pumpkin
Harry the Hedgehog and the Fireworks
Harry the Hedgehog's Christmas Cheer

www.ingramcontent.com/pod-product-compliance
Lightning Source LLC
Chambersburg PA
CBHW042313280426
43661CB00101B/1226